Pebble® Plus

Famous Firsts

THE FIRST AIRPLANES

by Megan Cooley Peterson

Consulting Editor: Gail Saunders-Smith, PhD

Consultant: Jonson Miller, PhD
Associate Teaching Professor of History and Science,
Technology, and Society
Drexel University

CAPSTONE PRESS
a capstone imprint

Pebble Plus is published by Capstone Press,
1710 Roe Crest Drive, North Mankato, Minnesota 56003
www.capstonepub.com

Library of Congress Cataloging-in-Publication Data
Peterson, Megan Cooley, author.
  The first airplanes / Megan Cooley Peterson.
     pages cm.—(Famous firsts)
  Summary: "Large photographs and simple text describe eight early airplanes"—Provided by publisher.
  Includes bibliographical references and index.
  ISBN 978-1-4914-0573-4 (hb)—ISBN 978-1-4914-0641-0 (pb)—ISBN 978-1-4914-0607-6 (eb)
1. Airplanes—Juvenile literature. 2. Airplanes—History—Juvenile literature. I. Title.
  TL547.P4224 2015
  629.133'34—dc23   2014001800

Editorial Credits
Erika L. Shores, editor; Terri Poburka, designer; Svetlana Zhurkin, media researcher; Laura Manthe, production specialist

Photo Credits
Alamy: Interfoto, 9, ITAR-TASS Photo Agency, 13; Corbis: Museum of Flight, 15; Library of Congress, cover, 7, 11; Newscom: akg-images, 17, 19; Shutterstock: Chris Parypa Photography, 21, IM_photo, 5

Note to Parents and Teachers

The Famous Firsts set supports national social studies standards related to science, technology, and society. This book describes and illustrates the first airplanes. The images support early readers in understanding the text. The repetition of words and phrases helps early readers learn new words. This book also introduces early readers to subject-specific vocabulary words, which are defined in the Glossary section. Early readers may need assistance to read some words and to use the Table of Contents, Glossary, Read More, Internet Sites, Critical Thinking Using the Common Core, and Index sections of the book.

Printed in the United States of America in North Mankato, Minnesota.
032014   008087CGF14

Table of Contents

The First Airplanes

Zoom! Airplanes soar
through the clouds. They take
people where they need to go.
Hitch a ride in the world's
first airplanes.

First Flight

Wilbur and Orville Wright built the Flyer. It was the first airplane to fly with a person on board. The Flyer flew for 12 seconds. It traveled 120 feet (37 meters).

The Wright brothers make the first successful airplane flight.

1903

Monoplanes

In 1907 Louis Blériot flew one of the earliest monoplanes. It had only one set of wings. Today most planes are monoplanes.

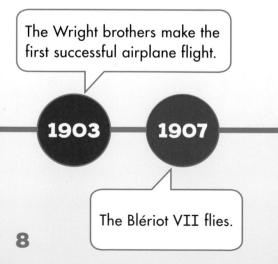

The Wright brothers make the first successful airplane flight.

1903　　**1907**

The Blériot VII flies.

Flying Boats

The F-boat was the first flying boat. Glenn Curtiss gave the plane's body a boat shape. F-boats flew for the U.S. Navy and Army.

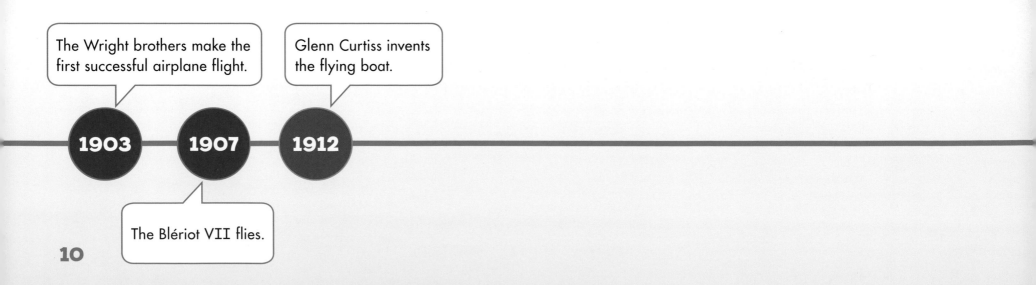

The Wright brothers make the first successful airplane flight.

Glenn Curtiss invents the flying boat.

1903   **1907**   **1912**

The Blériot VII flies.

Four-Engine Airplanes

Igor Sikorsky made history
when he built the Grand.
It was the first airplane
with four engines.

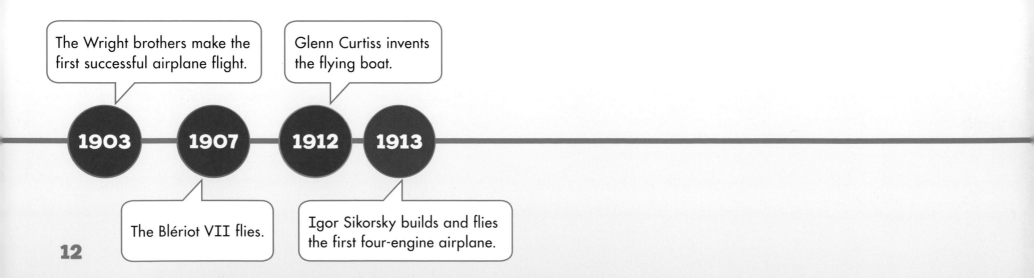

The Wright brothers make the first successful airplane flight.

Glenn Curtiss invents the flying boat.

1903 **1907** **1912** **1913**

The Blériot VII flies.

Igor Sikorsky builds and flies the first four-engine airplane.

Metal Planes

Hugo Junkers' Junkers J 1 was the first all-metal airplane. Metal planes are stronger than early wooden and fabric planes.

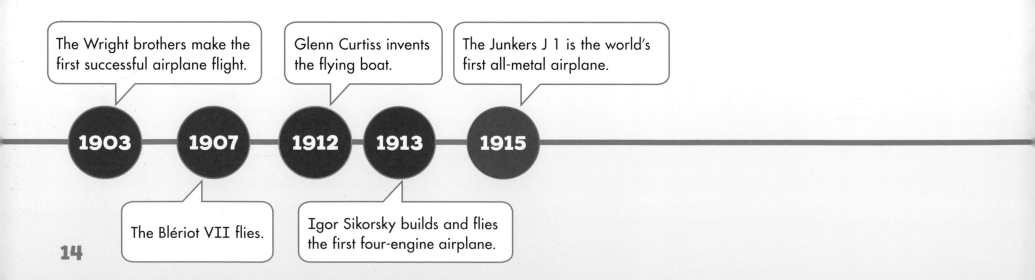

The Wright brothers make the first successful airplane flight.

Glenn Curtiss invents the flying boat.

The Junkers J 1 is the world's first all-metal airplane.

1903   **1907**   **1912**   **1913**   **1915**

The Blériot VII flies.

Igor Sikorsky builds and flies the first four-engine airplane.

67

Junkers

Jet Airplanes

The Heinkel He 178 could fly more than 400 miles (644 kilometers) per hour. It was the first jet plane.

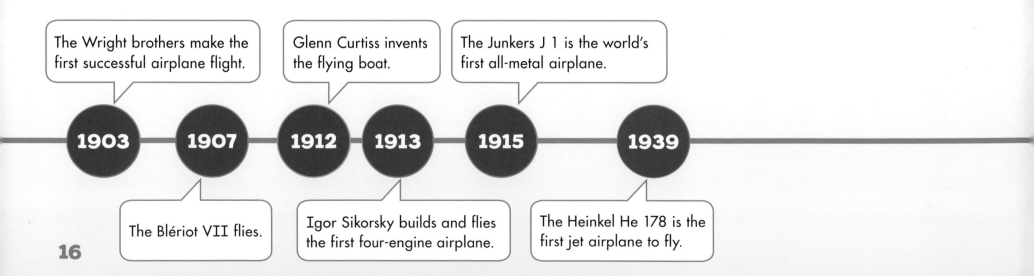

The Wright brothers make the first successful airplane flight.

Glenn Curtiss invents the flying boat.

The Junkers J 1 is the world's first all-metal airplane.

1903 1907 1912 1913 1915 1939

The Blériot VII flies.

Igor Sikorsky builds and flies the first four-engine airplane.

The Heinkel He 178 is the first jet airplane to fly.

Jet Fighters

The Messerschmitt Me 262 was the first jet combat plane. It flew about 550 miles (885 km) per hour.

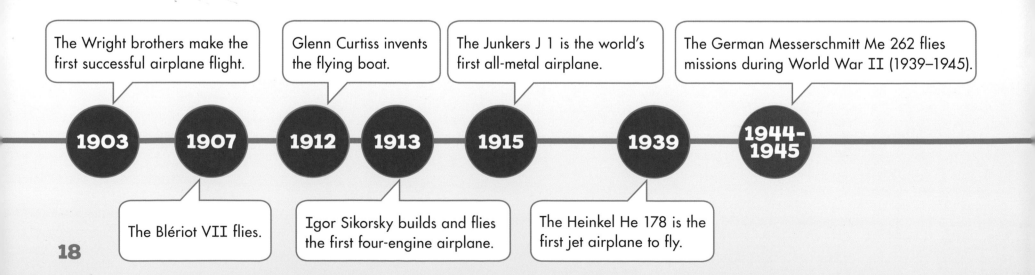

The Wright brothers make the first successful airplane flight.

Glenn Curtiss invents the flying boat.

The Junkers J 1 is the world's first all-metal airplane.

The German Messerschmitt Me 262 flies missions during World War II (1939–1945).

1903 **1907** **1912** **1913** **1915** **1939** **1944–1945**

The Blériot VII flies.

Igor Sikorsky builds and flies the first four-engine airplane.

The Heinkel He 178 is the first jet airplane to fly.

Jumbo Jets

Airplanes grew larger as more people traveled by air. The Boeing 747 held up to 490 passengers. This first jumbo jet had 6 million parts!

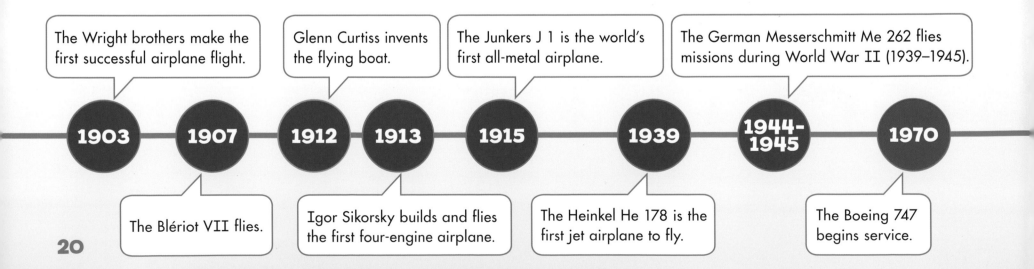

The Wright brothers make the first successful airplane flight.

Glenn Curtiss invents the flying boat.

The Junkers J 1 is the world's first all-metal airplane.

The German Messerschmitt Me 262 flies missions during World War II (1939–1945).

1903 · **1907** · **1912** · **1913** · **1915** · **1939** · **1944–1945** · **1970**

The Blériot VII flies.

Igor Sikorsky builds and flies the first four-engine airplane.

The Heinkel He 178 is the first jet airplane to fly.

The Boeing 747 begins service.

Glossary

combat—fighting between people or armies

engine—a machine that makes the power needed to move something

fabric—cloth or material

jet—an airplane with powerful engines

monoplane—a type of plane with one set of wings

Read More

Abramovitz, Melissa. *Military Airplanes.* Military Machines. Mankato, Minn.: Capstone Press, 2012.

Schaefer, Lola M. *Airplanes in Action.* Transportation Zone. Mankato, Minn.: Capstone Press, 2012.

Silverman, Buffy. *How Do Jets Work?* How Flight Works. Minneapolis: Lerner Publications, 2013.

Internet Sites

FactHound offers a safe, fun way to find Internet sites related to this book. All of the sites on FactHound have been researched by our staff.

Here's all you do:

Visit *www.facthound.com*

Type in this code: 9781491405734

Check out projects, games and lots more at
www.capstonekids.com

Critical Thinking Using the Common Core

1. Look at the photos on page 7 and page 21. Describe ways in which airplanes have changed over time. (Integration of Knowledge and Ideas)

2. What is one reason most airplanes are made out of metal now rather than wood and fabric? (Key Ideas and Details)

Index

Word Count: 200
Grade: 1
Early-Intervention Level: 19